Learning Points

Look at the pictures together and point to the words as you read them.

Encourage your child to talk about his/her teddy bear, umbrella, the cow you saw from the train window yesterday…

Ask simple questions – what noise do telephones make? When do you put your pyjamas on?

Play spot the colour. Every picture contains something blue. Look for this together and for blue things at home and outside.

Encourage your child to behave like a real reader and to read the book to you and to his/her teddies!

Acknowledgment
The publishers would like to thank Maureen Hallahan
for the hand lettering used in this book.

A catalogue record for this book is available
from the British Library

Published by Ladybird Books Ltd Loughborough Leicestershire UK
Ladybird Books Inc Auburn Maine 04210 USA

my first blue
picture
book

illustrated by JOHN DILLOW

teddy bear

duck

rocket

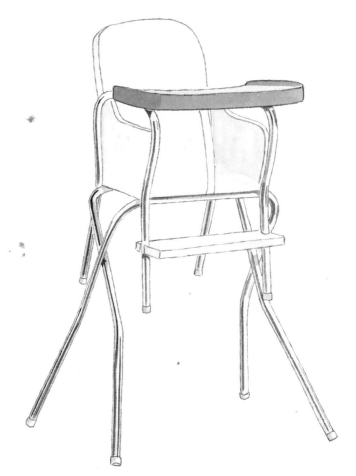

high chair

radio

kettle

pyjamas

puppet

telephone

COW

umbrella

playpen

fish

helicopter

bell

lamp

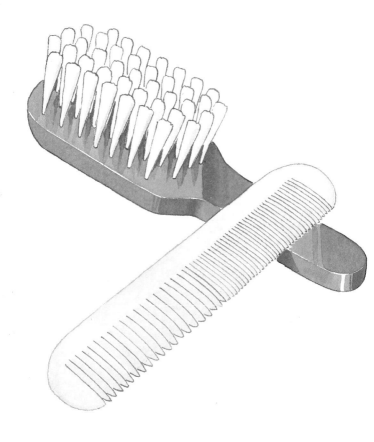

brush and
comb

paint box

sweater

purse

wheelbarrow

flag

engine

cup